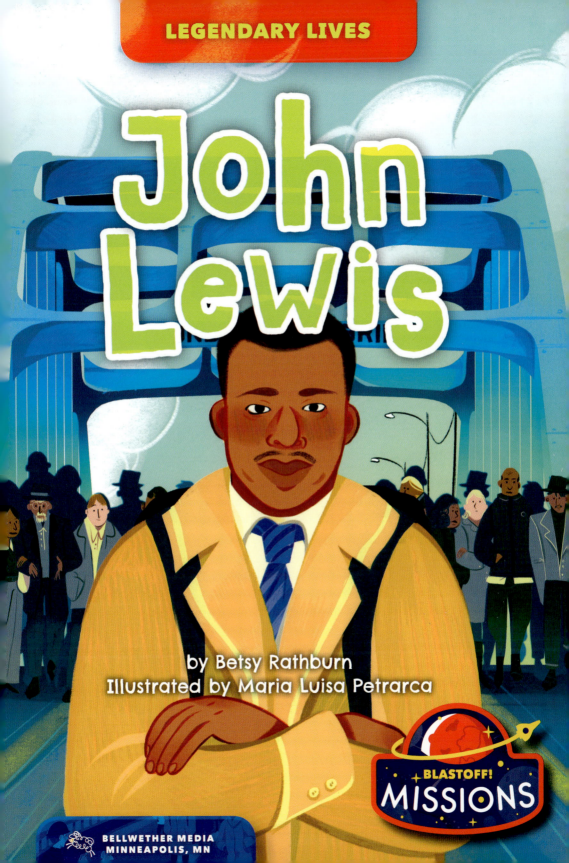

Blastoff! Missions takes you on a learning adventure! Colorful illustrations and exciting narratives highlight cool facts about our world and beyond. Read the mission goals and follow the narrative to gain knowledge, build reading skills, and have fun!

Traditional Nonfiction

Narrative Nonfiction

Blastoff! Universe

MISSION GOALS

> FIND YOUR SIGHT WORDS IN THE BOOK.

> LEARN ABOUT THE LIFE OF JOHN LEWIS.

> LEARN ABOUT HOW JOHN LEWIS FOUGHT FOR CIVIL RIGHTS.

This edition first published in 2025 by Bellwether Media, Inc.

No part of this publication may be reproduced in whole or in part without written permission of the publisher. For information regarding permission, write to Bellwether Media, Inc., Attention: Permissions Department, 6012 Blue Circle Drive, Minnetonka, MN 55343.

Library of Congress Cataloging-in-Publication Data

LC record for John Lewis available at: https://lccn.loc.gov/2024041931

Text copyright © 2025 by Bellwether Media, Inc. BLASTOFF! MISSIONS and associated logos are trademarks and/or registered trademarks of Bellwether Media, Inc.

Editor: Rebecca Sabelko   Designer: Andrea Schneider

Printed in the United States of America, North Mankato, MN.

This is **Blastoff Jimmy**! He is here to help you on your mission and share fun facts along the way!

Table of Contents

Meet John Lewis	4
An Early Start	6
Fighting for Freedom	10
A Great Leader	20
Glossary	22
To Learn More	23
Beyond the Mission	24
Index	24

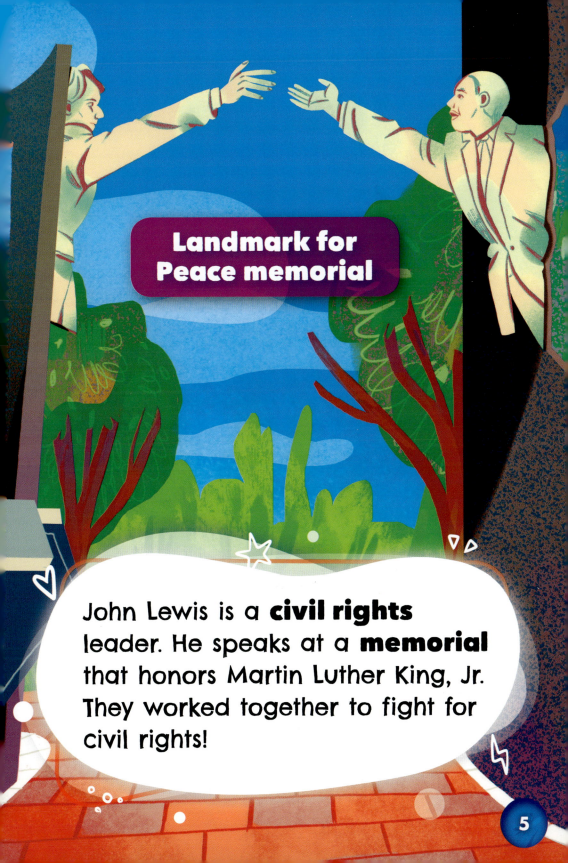

Landmark for Peace memorial

John Lewis is a **civil rights** leader. He speaks at a **memorial** that honors Martin Luther King, Jr. They worked together to fight for civil rights!

An Early Start

It is the 1940s. Young John lives in Alabama. His family is very poor.

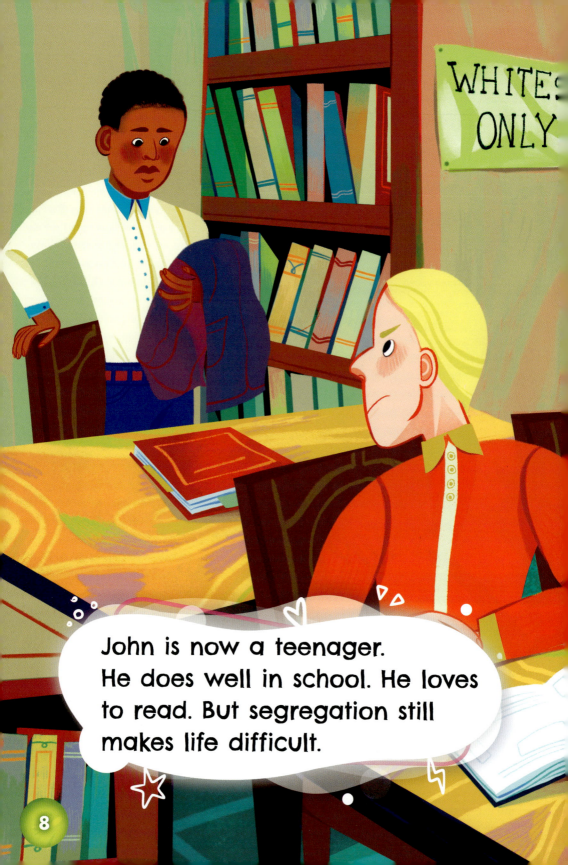

John is now a teenager. He does well in school. He loves to read. But segregation still makes life difficult.

Fighting for Freedom

Now John is a college student in Tennessee. Public places in his city are segregated. He is at a **sit-in**. Police **arrest** him for this **protest**. But he will not stop fighting for **equality**.

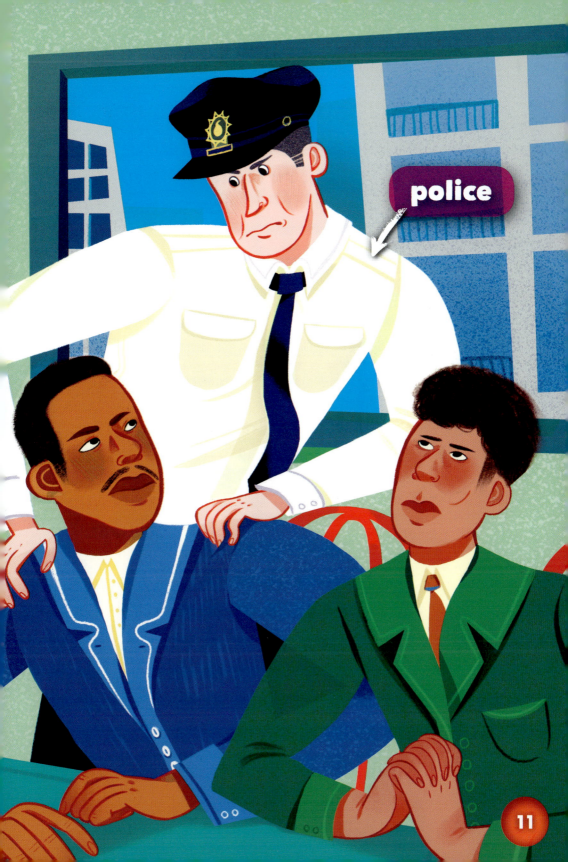

John is a **Freedom Rider**. He rides buses to fight for equality.

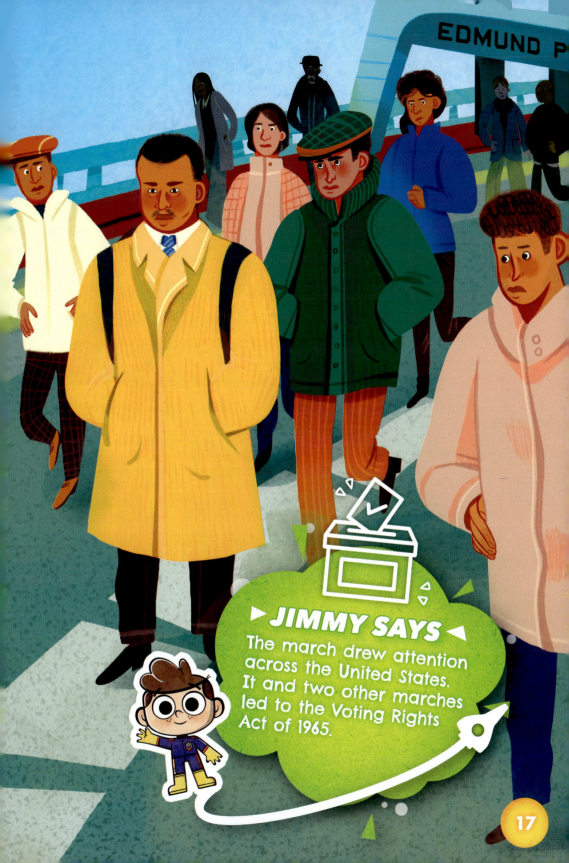

A Great Leader

Presidential Medal of Freedom

John is being honored by President Barack Obama. He receives the Presidential Medal of Freedom.

His work improved the lives of Americans. His fight for freedom lives on!

John Lewis Profile

Born
February 21, 1940, near Troy, Alabama

Died
July 17, 2020

Accomplishments

Leader during the Civil Rights Movement in the 1960s who later became a congressman in the U.S. House of Representatives

Timeline

1961: Travels through the South as a Freedom Rider

August 28, 1963: Gives a speech at the March on Washington for Jobs and Freedom

March 7, 1965: Leads the march from Selma to Montgomery, Alabama

January 3, 1987: Begins his first of 17 terms in the U.S. House of Representatives

February 15, 2011: Receives the Presidential Medal of Freedom

Glossary

arrest–to place under police control

civil rights–the rights all people have to freedom and equal treatment under the law

congressman–a member of the United States House of Representatives

demands–strongly asks for something

equality–just and fair treatment for all groups of people

Freedom Rider–a person who challenged racial laws in the South in the 1960s

immigrants–people who come from one country to live in another

memorial–a statue or building that honors a person or event

protest–an act to show that people are against something

represents–speaks for

segregation–the act of keeping groups of people apart based on race

sit-in–a protest in which people refuse to leave a place until their demands are met

To Learn More

AT THE LIBRARY

Green, Meghan. *The Story of the American Civil Rights Movement.* Buffalo, N.Y.: Cavendish Square Publishing, 2024.

Howell, Izzi. *Martin Luther King, Jr.* New York, N.Y.: Crabtree Publishing Company, 2021.

Hubbard, Crystal. *Who Was John Lewis?* New York, N.Y.: Penguin Workshop, 2023.

ON THE WEB

FACTSURFER

Factsurfer.com gives you a safe, fun way to find more information.

1. Go to www.factsurfer.com.

2. Enter "John Lewis" into the search box and click 🔍.

3. Select your book cover to see a list of related content.

BEYOND THE MISSION

> WHAT FACT FROM THE BOOK DID YOU THINK WAS THE MOST INTERESTING?

> WHAT DOES BEING A LEADER LOOK LIKE TO YOU?

> WHY DO YOU THINK JOHN LEWIS WAS A STRONG CIVIL RIGHTS LEADER?

Index

Alabama, 6, 16
buses, 12, 13
civil rights, 5, 9
congressman, 19
equality, 10, 13, 19
Freedom Rider, 13
Georgia, 19
King, Martin Luther, Jr., 5, 9, 15
march, 15, 16, 17
March on Washington, 15
memorial, 5
Obama, Barack, 20
Parks, Rosa, 9
police, 10, 11, 16
Presidential Medal of Freedom, 20
profile, 21
protest, 10
segregation, 7, 8, 10, 12
sit-in, 10
teenager, 8, 9
Tennessee, 10
voting rights, 16, 17
Voting Rights Act of 1965, 17